MW01592355

After Many Million Heartbeats

(make the title come alive)

(1) Title means something

(2) Rythm is everything.

(3) All metaphors
similes etc...
figures of speech etc.
<u>Understand</u> !

(4)

After Many Million Heartbeats

MYRTLE MARIE MARMADUKE

PEREGRINE SMITH BOOKS
SALT LAKE CITY

First edition

93 92 91   5 4 3 2 1

This is a Peregrine Smith Book, published by
Gibbs Smith, Publisher
P.O. Box 667
Layton, UT 84041

Design by Robin Johnson
Illustration by Shauna Clinger

Manufactured in the United States of America

**Library of Congress Cataloging-in-Publication
Data**
Marmaduke, Myrtle.
After many million heartbeats / Myrtle
Marmaduke.
   p.   cm.
  ISBN 0-87905-396-8 (pbk.)
  I. Title.
  PS3563.A676A69   1991
  811'.54—dc20   91-13157
                       CIP

*To Sam Marmaduke, Bonnie Alkire,
and Vernon Marmaduke*

Contents

Foreword

Mrs. Marmaduke is a spry ninety-two years old at this writing, but in spite of her age, she is an extremely lively conversationalist. Her memory is clear and has the power to move her emotionally as she recalls experiences from her childhood and young womanhood.

She was born in 1898 in Carthage, Missouri, but lived almost her entire life in Colorado. The grandchild of a Kentucky country school teacher and the child of a gold miner, she was raised with her brother and sister in Cripple Creek, Colorado. Due to a severe illness as a child, she admits that she was spoiled by her parents. One of her most vivid childhood recollections is of her first exposure to poetry. Although she can no longer remember the author of the poem "Somebody's Mother," she recalls that this poem first inspired her toward the vocation of poet at a mere eight years of age. With a twinkle in her eyes, she admits to having plagiarized the poem for a school recitation. As a result of her exposure to this poem, she says, "I am still writing poetry."

Her first job after high-school graduation in 1916 placed her in a one-room county schoolhouse in a rural Wyoming community. She recalls that not much formal learning took place there. "Mostly, the children and I played games." Later she married an accountant who was her companion for 55 years. They had a son and a daughter.

The forms of poetry that most appeal to Mrs. Marmaduke are the ballad, because of its tone and rhythm, and the sonnet, because of its technical aspects. She singles out "The Ballad of Reading Jail," by Oscar Wilde, as one of her favorite poetic works. She enjoys the free flow of lyric poetry and the structure of iambic pentameter. Her favorite authors are Edna St. Vincent Millay and Oscar Wilde.

Mrs. Marmaduke's own poetry is inspired by the beauties of nature and the affairs of the heart. Love is a main theme of her poetry. She feels that it is the days in our lives when we are in love that recall the greatest joys to our minds. In a sense, we are parasites of love; we live off love long after the corporeal presence of the loved person has departed. And that is why nostalgia clings to her love poems. While love imparts the greatest joys, it also "tortures us. When in love, we are jealous of the moments that the object of our love is away from us. That is pain."

Human tragedy, lost love, omissions of love, being touched by other people's pain, the hopelessness and helplessness of human existence, "failing to love when I wish I had loved," are other major themes of Marmaduke's poetry. As she puts it, "The heart is what matters. My poetry gets to the heart as well as to the heart of things. It deals with truth." It is easy for the poet to be truthful; it is much harder to know what truth is.

The poetry of Myrtle Marmaduke is also endowed with optimism and humor. Her poetry is multidimensional and multifaceted. Ranging from nature observation through cosmological speculation, from the power, joy, and sorrow of love through the profundities of the most complex questions that life poses to us all, she brings surprising insights and fresh images to our understanding.

K. Michael Seibt

After Many Million Heartbeats

Held Breath

Seeking, I found;
    and so, wide-listening, lay at the heart of all—
      an instant—an eternity—who knows?
I lay at the heart of the world and heard the world
    from creation to creation
    from forever to forever
    from now to now.
I heard the seas let forth; the great peaks rise;
    the sun burst red across the first day's rim;
      and in the churning fogs I heard it set.
I heard the mists rise over forming plains;
I heard the towering trees take root and shape;
I heard the spirit quiver and divide
    and scintillate in multiplicity;
I heard the ego enter into flesh.
Deep in the dark and dazzle of the mists
    I heard the heartbreak of divided soul;
      I heard the teardrops of the spirit flow.
Holding my breath, I heard the breath of things
    too near to fathom and too far to change.
I heard love turn to scarlet; truth to beige;
    peace turn to saffron; loyalty to gray.

——————————————

I heard the flame creep on the fleshly wall;
  I heard the smoke drift out across the sky;
    I heard the fiery embers dim and die
      and,
        soft as silence,
          heard the ashes fall.

Late Aura

Over the lonely meadows, falling snow
Whitens the shadows, spreading wings of light,
Feathering each hollow, casting up a glow
Ancient and mellow on the dark of night.
Softer than moonbeams shines this tender mood
After the weight of winter freeze has lifted;
A gentle cover for the solitude,
A mantle over scarred earth sweetly drifted.
Late in the darkest hour of night it falls,
Light to the darkness, memoried as clover;
Blithesome when unblithe winter lays its palls;
Blossom when summer blossomtime is over.
A field holds bleakness with the summer past
Till through the darkness comes the snow at last.

Concert at Red Rocks

Chalice of rock upon the mountain side,
stained with the ancient red of holiness,
it draws the multitudes from far and wide
to drink its living draught of loveliness.
The whir of man resounds upon its rim.
It feels the imprint of his eager feet.
Here, music pouring forth is life to him—
the warmth, the solace and the quickening beat.
It pours its wine upon the mountain air,
the deep bouquet, the flavor of its tone.
From this great cup of God, powerful as prayer,
streams forth an inspiration all its own—
red wine of music mixed with sunset dye
spilling its glory on the western sky.

Scent of Clover

When I was a long-legged, skinny, little girl,
We lived in a house by a field of clover;
In the blaze of the sun and the dew of the night
I loved it and I loved it, over and over.

Lonely it was in its white and scented beauty,
Lonely and lovely as train whistles were;
A skinny, little, long-legged girl could not
    express it—
But O, how it plucked at the heart of her!

The years have passed and the dreams have
    wilted,
But the far train whistles and the sweet and
    blowing clover
Stir from my long-legged, skinny, lovely child-
    hood
And pluck at the same heart—over and over.

Autumn Fires

How bright the bonfires of my childhood days
As summer drifted deeply into fall!
The chill, the burning leaves, the fragrant haze
Made this the most enchanting time of all.
We dipped dry sticks into the hungry fire
And leaped, and split the quiet with our screams.
Small, earth-kissed gypsies in ragshag attire,
We were knee-deep in life and leaves and
    dreams.
Leaf flame—wind-tousled gypsies—filmy skies—
I view this scene as one who stands apart.
A drift of pungent smoke still smarts my eyes—
(Or can a childhood memory twist the heart?)
The leaves, the scarlet flame, the haze-soft sun,
And youth's bright, blowing dreams all blur, as
    one.

Baskets to Fill

Earth gave us baskets, bidding each to fill
With fruits or flowers or what his dream
    conveyed.
We gathered pinks, my love and I, until
We reached the mountainside and there I
    stayed
Gathering sweet wild fern and columbine—
But he was scaling to the mountain's height!
What could he pluck above the timberline?
I dropped my flowers and cried to him in
    fright.

Earth clapped a hand across my frightened
    scream
And told me I must let my loved one go,
For each must pick according to his dream;
So he must climb and I must stay below.

My love returned, bruised, torn, and marked
    with scars,
And handed Earth his basket—filled with stars!

Of Things Not Seen

My winter elm tree stands with arms outspread
just as it stood in summer's glistening leaf.
Its grace and beauty are not past and dead;
it suffers from no loss and knows no grief.
It keeps its branches curved for loveliness,
for sun and shower, for birds that build and sing.
During the winter's icy stain and stress
it calmly reaches upward toward the spring.
So does the soul stand in its barren hour
amid the bitter blasts a winter long,
held ever upward toward the time of flower,
awaiting unseen leaf and latent song.
Some springtime force must keep its loved one
    whole—
sap of the tree—bright substance of the soul!

Birth of a Dream

From the hills, across the meadow
Blows a whisper sheathed in shadow,
Scented from some piney lane,
Muted, moody and alone;
Palid ray from misty night,
Sleepy stir of dawn's first note.

Little ray of palest amber,
Little wind still touched with slumber,
Fiercely, fiercely rouse your burning!
Blow the sky across the morning!
Rise above the yearning meadow
Scarlet-winged, flame-purged of shadow!

Borderland

The nerves lean outward from a day-wracked
    mind
to touch the shadowed stillness of the night,
to stretch, to sink, to steep in old delight,
familiar, loved, unutterably kind.
A tender stillness flows from far away,
swelling, like music, from some ancient sphere
to mist and mesmerize the midnight ear
until all memory seems to swirl and sway.
It drifts, perhaps, to Eden's hallowed dawn
of dew-wet grass and glossy shimmering leaf
before man's passion and his self-made grief
had caused his paradise to be withdrawn.
Before it reaches sleep, the mind drops free
into a momentary breath of bliss—
a glimpse, primeval, pure, untouched. And this
is not a dream. It is reality.

Remember Them Fair

This wind is the color of autumn leaves and sun,
    glinting copper and gold.
How many springs the wind was the color of
    apple blossoms,
      with wet lilacs laced into its perfume!
I remember when the wind was red roses at
    midnight;
and again the sapphire of cold,
    glittering with new snow and stars.
There was a time—and a time—and a time—
when the wind was rain, and it was the color of
    tears
    and the glisten of teardrops—
when it was a black shroud swirling out of
    the pit of night—
when it was a gray mist blowing over an empty
    dawn—
Heart, be still! If you must remember winds,
    remember them fair!

And a Hill to Climb

I am no continent. My small terrain,
From bird's-eye view, is pleasant field and stream;
Soft threads embroidering a pastoral theme—
Soft sun, soft wind and softly warming rain
Shimmering to life the gently growing grain.
But those who know it realize its scheme
Holds also falling star and dying dream,
And storms that sweep across it, hill and plain.

Some dawns unroll the sunrise that I seek;
Some sunsets spill their gold on cloudless air;
Sometimes the grasses sing, the boulders speak,
And honeyed winds breathe blossoms in my hair.
High in the mist I see my shining peak.
I have not climbed it yet. But it is there.

Sovereign by Grace

If a tree can be grotesque, this was the one,
a great gray giant, stark against the sky,
splintered limbs rough and bleached by many
    a sun,
scant foliage, meager shade for passersby.
And yet, birds flocked to grace its waiting arms—
bright-winged, sweet-throated, they would nest
    and sing.
The tree, long used to borrowed grace and
    charms,
held court as regally as any king.
It stood, gaunt-limbed, thin-robed, the summer
    long
haloed with color, symphonied with song.

Midsummer Rain

The rain came pouring suddenly last night
Before the drooping land was quite aware.
I felt the quickening of the earth's delight;
I heard excited whisperings on the air
As withered blade and listless flower and tree
Reached forth to drink its fill of ecstasy.

I rose today to greet the usual dawn
And found the scene transformed before my
    eyes
For though the wild, impulsive rain had gone,
It left the lingering thrill of its surprise.
The earth lay quivering in a rosy light,
Remembering kisses it had had last night.

The Mistress

I am not kith nor kin nor beauty's choice;
I trot, self-willed, as one of beauty's slaves.
I leap to catch the echo of her voice;
I chase the atoms scattered when she waves;
I gulp the teardrops dripping from her mist;
I embrace the air left vacant by her wings.
I am a jaw to stop her satin fist.
I am a sound board stretched beneath her
    strings.
O, I have crept into her lap at night
Feeling her nestle earth and me as one;
And I have followed her through dawn's dim
    light
And watched as she exploded into sun.
Her seeking hand caresses small and great;
She hangs the stars; she tints the flower's cup;
Yet never think that she will hesitate
To stab, to strangle, sear or swallow up.
She loves to split a heart like mine in two,
Widening the wound to ride a full moon
    through!

The Garden

The roses bloom and blend their myriad hues
In rose togetherness and rose delight;
Together glowing in the morning dews,
Together blowing in the sweet of night.
The heedful gardener knows how each, alone,
Sought, through the dark, the fingers of the sun
And how each petal unfolded to its own—
Each rose full-borning, one by one by one.
And when the time of scent and hue is past,
When winds grow harsh and urgent in their call,
When all must weaken in their hold as last
And all must wither and let go and fall,
The mindful gardener in his wisdom knows
The letting-go comes, lonely, to each rose.

Pegasus

It is not a wood; and nor is it a pasture—
it is a sloping greenland graced with trees
on one side only. The large expanse flows free,
     and wide to willful wind and sun.
It was here that I first saw him resting in shade,
a sleek and slender creature, young, as young
     as very dawn.
"He must be a gift to me," I thought, "This is my
     land."
And yet I dared not touch him. I would only stay
    a bit aside, breathing the air he breathed.
Times thereafter, I would gaze at him
     racing in sun and shadow
     breeze-tossed or serene.
     Sometimes a glow of gold,
     a streak of silver,
even, at times, a grim and ghostly gray.

But once, without a thought of him, I wandered
alone and lonely in the midnight moonlight
    heart-hurt with broken love.
He came, unasked. He came to me and touched
     my hand.
How tenderly I stroked his satiny beauty.
It was a vow, a subtle vow, wind-witnessed.
Time only, can unfold these fragile things.
We knew, at last that both of us had wings.

Philosophical View

The mountain stands against the sky
In regal splendor, strong and high
Attesting its nobility
While on the plain the grasses bend
And dance and play the days on end
In uttermost futility
The lofty mountain far surpasses
All attributes of silly grasses
With their inane docility
But grasses have such fun, whereas
It seems to me a mountain has
Just grim responsibility

Solitary Flight

White are the reaches of the soul,
Longing and lonely and alone;
Searching the earth from pole to pole,
Calling through space to find its own.

And its empty echoes answer back
From the cliffs and crags and the hanging
    skies,
Daring to mock the bitter lack
Ringing out in the soul's wild cries.

The surface green is the heart's release,
A little of life's unmeasured breath;
And the heart accepts and calls it peace—
But the soul must have all of life, or death.

A heart takes a crumb and a fireside berth,
And smiles and clings to its precious mite;
But a soul goes outward across the earth
Crying and calling through the night.

The Dream Defiled

A ball of fire hurled, thundering, into space
by some all-powerful, never-erring hand
slowed gently, gently cooled in ageless mist,
softened in tender green upon its face,
spread into ocean, ripened into land,
flushed dawn's soft rose, glowed twilight's
    amethyst.
If not a heaven, it was heaven-kissed.
Then man was breathed to life and took
    command.
Blessed and endowed, but arrogant of birth,
he feels himself creation's master and
so slays, pollutes, uproots at awesome pace.
Proclaiming progress, he creates a dearth.
He may destroy his own beloved earth,
leaving but wind and ash to mark the place.

Of Birds and Things

He flitted through the branches of the tree
With flash of wings and pouring gold of throat.
Catlike I watched him. He was swift and free!
He thrilled my soul with every liquid note!
I knew he must be mine; and so I held
The iron cage and deftly lured him in.
He sat, a leaden creature, drooped and quelled,
His eyes closed tight in brooding and chagrin.
The cage was large but still he would not fly
Nor preen a feather. He had lost the wine
That spilled in golden notes across the sky.
He simply sat there, now that he was mine.
The door was safely locked; the cage was strong;
But I had captured neither wings nor song.

Nocturne

Sleepless, I lean upon the deeps of night,
My heart wide-listening to its shaded tones—
The tinkling bells of silence, soft and light,
Mixed with the earth's small cries and anguished
    moans.
A yard dog's yearning bay of loneliness
Traces an echo somewhere in my heart;
One lone train whistle broods an old distress
Wailing "We meet to part—we meet to part."
I feel the great chords as I sink to sleep,
In diapason with the night's vast whole,
Proclaiming that eternity is deep
And earth too shallow to contain the soul.
Stretched on the staff of midnight's space and
    bars,
I breathe the music of both earth and stars.

The Dawn Burst Red

The roaring tides of cosmic fire had ceased;
eternal space stretched in a night of blue.
The worlds, so lately from their hell released,
turned in the fresh, sweet clouds of mist and dew
and dreamed new dreams of moderate delight
until their dreaming came to rest upon
some lambent ending to the shadowed night—
the gentle cast of something known as dawn.
Such dreams were pale! Swift, stabbing shafts of
    red
burst wide the darkness with exultant ray!
In all the worlds the gloom of night had fled
before the flaming glory of the day.
The great spheres swung and chimed in joyous
    key—
the morning bells across infinity!

Concerto

My hands have never touched a violin;
My fingers do not ache for string and bow;
Yet when its mighty tide comes surging in,
My heart has river beds to catch the flow.

Softly it moves as moonbeams on the night
Or summer clouds that shed their drops of rain;
The glistening waves now whisper young delight;
Now moan, to mark the heart's first stretch of
     pain.

The passions roar—the frenzied breakers leap—
The wind—the flash—the scream—the
     anguished roll!
The storm that thunders on this mighty deep
Is one with that which surges in the soul.

The current swells within my pounding breast,
Flooding, like memory, my thirsting veins.
It leaves that flotsam of a vast unrest;
Old heartbreak quivers in its dying strains.

Now mist lies purple on the lonely sea
And mist lies gray along the barren shore;
The waves, like tired tears, rise tenderly—
My rivers flow within their banks once more.

At the Fresh of Beginning

Yesterday, or a million yesterdays ago,
we were knee-deep in childhood;
we sisters and our little sister chums,
hair tightly pigtailed, faces freshly scrubbed,
our eyes stretched wide to drink each long, long
    day.
Springtime was such excitement, such allure!
Saturdays, free from school, we went flower
    hunting—
a contest, seeing who could gather most.
One Friday night the rain came down in torrents
and so next day our mothers thought the woods
would be too wet. But our broken hearts won out.
We went. And I remember how the woods
were secret, soaked and silent,
the tree trunks blackened, branches trickling
    green.

Each of us went her secret way alone,
Each so intent upon her gathering.
Deep, deep into the dripping woods I went
and suddenly before my dazzled eyes
I came upon the trunk of a giant tree
lying there rotting, sinking in the ground
and covered from end to end with violets;
bright, beautiful, spring fragrant violets.
Here life and death washed fresh, all mixed
    together
I stood and breathed the mystery of the woods
deep and ancient and rising from it all
the smell of growing, of blowing and of dying,
I stopped to pluck my find. My fingers froze.
What it was I felt I did not know,
But I breathed it into me to remain forever.

I rose and went my way over sodden ground
and came out of the woods at last in a splash of
    sunlight—
my hands empty of violets.
Soft sun, soft wind and softly warming rain
Shimmering to life the gently growing.

Witness

Once in a wasteland bare of flower or tree
I was a mute world lost in emptiness;
I was a heart unseen and tenantless
For nothing is, where there is none to see.
So I existed without entity.
No voice was mine to either mock or bless,
No thunder and no murmur of caress,
For where no listener is, no sound can be.
I was a region, bleak and set apart
Until you came and breathed upon my heart;
Then I was life; then I was tone and hue;
And I was entity, for someone knew.
You looked—and beauty blossomed all around!
You listened—and the whole world thrilled with
    sound!

No Standard Measure

Love, so definite and so uncontradictable,
    is yet prone to vagaries
        and full of contradictions.
Even the dimensions of love are variable;
    one moment outlining infinity
        filling the sky and the land
the next moment curled like a kitten purring
    soft and sweet in the hand.
Love found me and I found love and I lay
    in its night of mystery
and walked in its tossing dawn
    with its berries sweet on my tongue;
I stood on its towering peaks and beheld the
    world in its shimmer
and sipped from its golden goblet
    breaking my virgin fast.

Love was the world. Love was the goblet in my
   hand.
   Love was the wine I drank from the goblet.
Now love is dead.
No. No—love is not dead.
I still stand on its peaks and stare at the world
   for the world still is
but its shimmer is no longer there.
My hand still holds the goblet—tarnished cup—
   The wine on longer sweet
   no longer red.
O I sense the dimensions of love. As small as my
   hand.
   As small as a kitten purring.
As vast as the world in my eyes, seeming vaster
   and too far away through the blur
      in my eyes.
It is as round as tears. As flat as a bubble bursted.
   As many-cornered as a heartache.
I cannot mark the boundaries or keep the
   dimensions apart.
Except to know that a heartache can be wider
   than the heart.

Blow Me a Heartbreak

Lilac my heart with love again
With fragrance of spring and kisses
With throb of joy, with thump of pain
With face raised to the splash of rain—
All these the now dream misses.

April again my tingling flesh
Wild-berry my joyous tongue
Trap me in lilac's misty mesh
Blow me a heartbreak wild and fresh
And young! and young! and young!

Windsweep the fog from dull, brown days
Toss me an earth that quakes
Light me with lovely lilac blaze
Shatter my heart a million ways
But catch it as it breaks!

Enchanted Silence

First love need have no words.
No word, no volume ever could express
Such vast of tenderness.
It steals like mist on that unfolding hour
And it is shyness, holiness and power,
Hushed, lest if spoken it might disappear.
Its perfume tints the air like ancient musk,
A flower's shadow stirring in the dusk
And in its depth the shadow of a tear.
It is a moon-wind tossing in the night,
Fragile, illumined, awesome in its flight;
Blowing the widening heart beyond its bars
To climb the sky and tremble through the stars.

Handkerchief

Lacy, scented, small, white square,
Crumpled up and lying there,
What a secret trust you bear!

Dark-fringed eyes of gentian blue
Gave their anguished tears to you;
Trembling fingers wound you through.

Till the first faint streaks of light
You gave comfort as you might—
You were all she had last night.

Dainty trifle spun of thread,
You have helped a heart weep red;
You have felt a love bleed dead.

You'll forget the tears you hide;
You'll be cleansed and purified,
Pressed, perfumed, restored to pride.

———————————

What about the love that died?

Second Honeymoon

These were the hills that witnessed the first flush
of their young love when they were newly wed.
The gentle morning rains, the twilight hush,
the sunsets when the clouds were dipped in red—
all memoried moments. Now they have returned
to try to catch again the throb and thrill
of bright, fresh-kindled fires that in them burned
when they were new to life and greening still.

Tonight, their embered fire is hot and bright
in readiness to cook the evening meal.
Working, they touch with love, accustomed, right,
more precious than the springtime thrill, more real.
The fires of youth are rampant, wild and fleet,
but autumn fires burn steadfastly and sweet.

The Secret Way

Stretch not. Love is high;
Too high to be reached.
Bend not. Love is deep;
Too deep to be sounded.
Speed not. Love is swift;
Too swift to be caught.
Scheme not. Love is wise;
It cannot be confounded.

But wait! Keep a candle aglow in
    your dreaming;
Keep wings in your heart widely
    spreading and stout—
High love will come bending,
Deep love will come reaching,
Swift love will come speeding,
Wise love will come teaching—
All love will come searching and
    seeking you out!

Midnight Wine

Shimmer of moonlight on the quivering grass,
Breath of red roses on the night-dewed air;
Young leaves reach out to touch me as I pass—
O, what a night for love to fill the glass
If I but had a lover waiting there!

My well-lived heart is just a little sad,
For beauty is too sweet to bear alone;
But all the countless moonlit nights I've had,
And all the kisses, tender, gay, and mad,
And all the lovely heartbreaks I have known

Glimmer like moonbeams in this heart of mine
And pearl the mist of years around my head.
I lift the glass, splashed with my foolish brine,
To those who drink of youth's unsalted wine
And dare to pluck the rose while it is red.

Finale

Train whistles fill the years with our goodbye—
Heart, earth and sky.
I walk again across that winter day
Wearing my star-filled eyes and rose-flushed face
And a velvet coat that caressed my neck with fur.
The snow-filled air was soft as gossamer
As your strong hand possessed my arm in its
    special way
And we passed through the end of the world at
    lovers' pace.
I rubbed my face against your rough, cold sleeve
Breathing your scent of tobacco and the clean,
    right smell
Of shaving lotion and man. The falling snow
Encrusted our lashes, softly feathered our hair.
At the sound of the train's oncoming bell
Emptiness tugged my heart but I brushed it
    aside—
The world brimmed over for our love was there.
The train waited, puffing. Suddenly your lips
Made a warm home to house my loneliness;
Opened a world of invulnerable loveliness.
We clung together gathering strength to part,
Clinging with lips and arms and fingertips,
Clinging with look and word and breath and
    heart.
We were parting for a little while, we thought.
We smiled, we waved, made lovers' secret signs,
No sorrowful word, no vague, prophetic sigh—
"Till we meet again," life said;
It was goodbye.

New Leaf

Yesterday is an orange, squeezed and dry;
It would be wise to throw the rind away.
An eaten fruit cannot tempt tongue nor eye;
We can but taste the plucked fruit of today.
And yet I've stored away dried rind and peel,
Nostalgic for the flavor of the past,
Some tender love to hold, some joy to feel—
The orange of yesterday, not meant to last.

A bright grove stretches far as eye can see,
Fragrance and fruit and tender, blowing leaf.
What are these hoarded, old, dried rinds to me
But memories of an emptied joy or grief?
O, let me take the path toward morning skies
Where laden, fresh tomorrows fill my eyes!

We'll All Pass

He sat at his table and played the game
With hands that were small and frail.
His face had been twisted with fright when he
    came;
He was forced through the doorway and
    tagged with a name,
And they paid no heed to his wail!

But his eyes grew used to the muted light
And the players at all their places.
It wasn't long till he lost his fright;
He learned to hold his cards just right
And to make the most of his aces.
The time went by, and his hands grew strong,
And his heart was lost in the game.
He played his cards, some right, some wrong—
He quite forgot he had played so long—
And it slipped his mind how he came.

The flush of youth was on his face
And the glint of youth in his hair;
He flipped his cards with a carefree grace—
He loved this room and he held his place
And played the game with an air.

The rose of his cheeks began to fade
And the gold left his hair at last;
He missed them at times but the bid must be
    made,
The tricks must be counted, the game must be
    played—
And the cards fell thick and fast.
There was once when he had a run of luck
So bad that he wasn't able
To keep his balance and show his pluck;
He told his friends he had run amuck—
And he slammed his cards on the table!
But they slapped him loudly on the back
And pushed him back in his place;

They told him luck couldn't be all black—
He must deal again from the same old pack
And keep that grin on his face.

So he played the game and his hair grew white
And his cheeks grew thin and old;
Again his face wore a look of fright;
He couldn't play his aces right;
And the cards were too heavy to hold.

They fell from his hand and he let them lie,
And tottered across the floor.
Some tried to stop him; some asked him why;
And others simply waved goodbye
As he wandered out the door.
Those at his table sat hushed and wan,
A question on every face—
Why had he wearied and wandered on?
When would they see him? Where had he
    gone?
And they stared at his empty place.

But a stranger, passing, saw it too,
And gaily sat down in it;
The cards were shuffled, the bid was new,
The trump was named, and the tricks just
    flew—
They had hardly lost a minute!

All the World's a Stage

We are not meant to understand the whole.
Each learns to act his lifetime, piece by piece
In sober conscience or in mad caprice;
So, as his lines read, each performs his role.
And some may ridicule and some console
If, wearied, some poor actor seeks release,
Or fate or folly deems his work must cease.
This does not mar the greatness of the soul.

How many scenes of laughter and of tears,
Some wise, some foolish as befits the part—
How many creaking curtains rise and fall
Before, worn out with acting down the years,
Each of us, reconciled within his heart,
Paints a brave face for his last curtain call!

Earth Lover

There's never a spring moon hung in the sky,
    And never a lilac blowing,
But I think of the day that I must die;
I know I must leave here by and by,
    And I have no will for the going.

Earth is a strife the coward flees,
    And heaven's a quiet place;
But I have a love for things like these:
A sudden wind in the waiting trees,
    And a wet leaf blown in my face.

O God, let heaven be not too still;
    My heart is so full of mirth!
Let my friends be gay and my birds sing
       shrill—
Or make me young again, if You will,
    For one more life on earth.

After Many Million Heartbeats

Of course I shall pass; there is evidence of this
    no mortal can deny—
What I said, and I say it again, is I will not die.
I shall gather the strings of whatever of earth
    I loved and tether them in my breast;
So when you have folded my hands and closed
    the lid, be not too sure that I rest,
For I may drift unexpectedly into this same
    music, pulling my strings in your heart
And a word, even the littlest word we have
    spoke may swing the curtains apart
And we shall be sitting together as we now sit,
    mingling our thoughts and our laughter
So you will not for long moments remind
    yourself I am part of what you call hereafter—
Most definitely in springtime, the smell of
    tansy dripping with rain
Will strike you dumb at the first breath,
    squeezing a little like pain.
Then you will say "It is you!" in an impulsive,
    maybe shocked, little cry
And I'll answer, grammatically as you always
    wished me to, "Yes, yes, it is I."
And I will move in your blood and warm it and
    you will know, however it be
That out of the impossible I have come to
    you—And will always come to you
That beyond all doubt it is me.

Test of Valor

Day ends—
The dark descends—
A soothing powder, deftly sifted.
By day the worlds of sky are hid
Beneath a tightly fitted lid;
At night the lid is lifted.

The huddled trees, foreboding, sigh
As night flings wide the endless sky—
Infinity—so wide—so high!
Beyond the rest, one lone tree sends
Its branches heavenward, and blends
Its soul with night. It needs no friends.

Could that proud spirit be my own
To stand out fearless and alone!
And yet if I should be a tree,
As in some distant dawn I may,
Let other trees stand close to me—
I'll need them there at close of day.

Dear Lord, I haven't courage, quite,
To stand alone against the night!

The Seed Remains

Lover of earth, your loves must disappear;
Your flowers must fade, your flames must die
    away.
The rosy winds and tides you hold most dear
Must vanish in a monotone of gray.
Yet, must this lie so heavy on the heart?
Each day dims into night, but comes the
    morning!
Bestow your kiss on all that must depart;
Garland it with your joy at its reborning.
The seed remains although the flower must
    die—
The flame burns out but fire will always be—
How wonderful to know that you and I
Go round and round in immortality!

Seasonal

That bare branch etched against the sky
Is not more stark and cold than I,
Is not more drab and gray.
My dreams were shattered, its leaves were blown;
My loves have vanished, its birds have flown;
The summer has passed away.

Dreams or leaves, does it matter at all?
The dreams must fade, the leaves must fall
And the summers must ever pass.
Hopes may be high and fresh as dawn
But the winds pass over and they are gone,
For the days of man are as grass.

Yet the way God works is a wonderful way!
Now the leaf is mold and the dream is clay
And the winter's a wasted thing;
But the green of newer leaves will shine,
And the heart's brave dreams will flow like
    wine —
Come spring!

Delayed Start

O, I have a mountain too
The same as you
Though I never leave the shelter of the plain
And spend my days, day long, among its grasses
As I watch you climb.
I renew my dream as each of you surpasses
The obstacles to scale your isolated peak
Daring great rockslides, braving wind and rain.
For me this is not the time.
Not yet will I seek
What lies up there where the moon is and the
    sunsets are,
Unembraced, unpossessed, aloof, rugged and
    high.
I see such change in your faces when the feat is
    done—
Tired with good weariness but set with pride,
Keen hunger gone, with fruits of the dream
    supplied.
I am going to start out soon—next day it may
    be—or next day but one—
But I mourn a little for you
That your dream is through
While my peak still stands untouched against
    the sky
With its undimmed star;
Unmatched, invincible, beautiful—
                    And far!

Follow the Wind

Stumbling through the hollows, groping
   through the mist,
Fighting on the hillsides, using heel and fist;
One will burn his candle to count a bag of
   gold;
One will journey barefoot to find a truth to
   hold.
This one sold an empire to buy a moment's
   bliss;
That one bled his heart out to steal a scarlet
   kiss.
While one there is who welters in leisure, lust,
   and lies,
One toils above a dying dream with starlight in
   his eyes.
Stumbling, groping, striding through fog and
   dust and dew,
Fighting, loving, bleeding a hell and heaven
   through—
The oceans cup our teardrops, our laughter
   rides the hills;
An April lilac blowing, the dream of spring
   fulfills.
Stretch, Seas, to hold our heartaches!
Hills, reach to catch our mirth!
Blow us your dreams, O April—
We need them here on earth!

Walk Through Grief

Black, black and dead this forest
And burned beyond their core the magnificent
    trees and all
the vines and flowers and little grasses
That once wove tenderness and their own soft
    witchery.
Is there no end to this? Are there no boundaries
Or is this a hopeless center lost in forever and I
    the only
life to bear it witness?
O, I have learned that hell is not a fire; hell is a
desolation where fire has been.
Fire has furious life and there is no life here.
    Except myself.
I am life and I stumble among the dead.
I shall stop right here, I say. I shall lie down
    where I am
and give up breathing and be no longer a witness.
For the millionth time I have said it, and for the
    millionth
        time I see
Beyond the mist, shimmering in early sun, a
    dripping bough
Blowing soft in the fresh of beginning—tenderly
    green.
I cry out "I am coming! Wait up! Wait up for
    me."
And so again strain forward.
My aloneness rises out of a greater aloneness.
My cry falls empty on echoing emptiness.
Can ever the rose of dawn break through such
    mist?
After the long, charred miles of stumbling and
    falling
Can I hope to arise in some brisk and rain-washed
    now
To clasp in my arms, at last, that wet and blowing
    bough?

Blown Seed

Do flurries of apple blossoms
    mist the wide and billowy meadows
        of eternity?
Do wet, spring lilacs,
    tossing in purple loveliness,
      sweeten forever's breath?
Do black wings
    shadow the cerulean brilliance
      of sky-arched immensity,
Leaving behind
    the swirling clouds of stifling, ash-gray
        death?
Do wild winds
    of destruction rush upon the pristine forests
      of the ancient alone,
Desolating
    the twilight green of solitude, stripping
      lashing and rending?
Do rivers flow like tears
    through the echoing caverns of moss-hung,
      eoned stone,
And churn
    like broken hearts over the cliffs
      of the never-ending?
There is a heart
    that pulses with holy love even as it rages
      in unholy vehemence.
There is a hand
    that mutilates the beautiful and beloved
      then tenderly ministers to its need.
Surely from one immortal source,
    from the very genes of omnipotence
      came forth this seed.

Somewhere, sometime, somehow,
    within the compassionate womb
        of perfect virginity
Sprang the seed
    of imperfect beginning, even
        this mortal birth.
It is heartbreak
    and dawn-rose and wind and the tender wash
        of divinity;
It is blowing blossom,
    bird shadows and tears, and a kiss
        on the mouth of infinity—
            it is earth!

Out of the Mists

Clean-husked and sweet, the cell of me has lain
Deep in the core of far, primordial dawn;
Part of the untried seed; one with awaiting;
One with the caught breath and the strange,
   new hunger
Quivering the vitals of a borning world.
I knew unfolding, knew the incipient stir
Of every dart of joy or prick of pain.
I saw, but no! I felt! I wholly helped
The ages form, the darkness gather light.
I, at the core, served at the quickening,
Suffered the birth, accepted and rejoiced!
But now, so long this ordered globe has spun
In form and fragrance and accustomed light
That I, a complacent cell, can scarce recall
The pre of dawn, that glorious, quaking start
When I lay, tender, at creation's heart.

Entity

The shadow leaps ahead or lags behind;
Seems individual; seems greater than;
Stretches the long-legged ego of its kind
Unlike its author's symmetry of plan.
It is an uncouth, dim imagining
Cutting a figure of great power and force,
A fleeting, floating, insubstantial thing
Lacking the noble outlines of its source.
And yet the shadow is forever chained
To its essential, something real and whole,
Just as our mortal being is contained
Within our own infinity of soul.
Beneath the broad forever of the sun
The shadow and its source move forth as one.

More Than I Ask

I ask for less;
God always gives me more.
I crave the little and the glittering things;
God gives me stronger and less shining wings
To carry me along a rockier shore.

I asked for beauty,
A youthful and heartbreaking loveliness
To place me at the center of the stage.
God took my soul and mellowed it with age
And taught it how to walk with loneliness.

I asked for power;
I wanted to be greater than the others.
God took my heart and made it understand
That I must take the lame ones by the hand
And say "I go your way for we are brothers."

I ask amiss.
I ask the earth-sweet way.
God knows forever at the very start
The workings of the mind and soul and heart.
I learn a very little day by day.

The Burden Bearer

Poor phantom creature, slow of mind and limb,
Devoid of wit, initiative or mirth,
You are OLD AGE with vision false and dim
Yet you are welcomed on the streets of earth.
We feed you as we place upon your back
Our sins of cowardice and failing might;
We shove our loss of will into your pack,
Our soft submission to the ease of night.
Our blunted swords, our plates of tarnished
    steel
You carry as you pass unsure and slow.
We sense, we reason that you are not real
And yet our sins outweigh you as you go
Bearing our dreams, unripened and ill-timed;
Crusades unfinished; mountains never climbed.

Taking Issue With An Adage

Be not deceived, the race *is* to the swift;
The plum is for the avid mouth and red.
The ones who get, both heaven and earth must
    lift!
Those who arrive keep forging on ahead!
Relax no effort, hold no power subdued,
Or it will fade and die before your eyes;
Your will must be renewed and yet renewed
If you would hold within your hands the prize.

O, keep your forces hidden if you will,
Like languid tigers ever crouched to spring;
Cover your eyes with slumberous lids until
The time is ripe—then leap! Then take!
    Then cling!
To grasp the prize, to clasp the golden gift,
Be not deceived,
    THE RACE *IS* TO THE SWIFT!

Myopia

From my own door I see a paradise
Shimmering in tender rose and misty green;
A luscious Eden waiting to entice
With lace of waterfall and flowering scene.
Yet it is but the dead-end of our street.
How well I know it—plain and commonplace!
My eyes, near-sighted, foster this deceit;
And, too, I have the sunset in my face.
An ordinary life may look as rare;
All rose and green, all endless, fountained fun
When with near-sighted, longing eyes we stare
Backward, against the rays of setting sun.
How sweet the echoes of the past may rise
Across our sunset-blurred, myopic eyes!

Dark Side of Dawn

I walked across the parable of dawn
Bursting the dark with joyous, shouting fire;
Breathing its tender, minted breath upon
The walking earth beneath, all things entire.
A dauntless presence rides the morning mists,
A new resolve that cannot be denied,
Charging with sparkling eyes and swinging fists
The sulk of night that would impede its ride.
I walked the parable of dawn and drew
Its blossoming breath as one despairing would;
Yet by the very joy of it I knew
Night surely must return. I understood.
How could the blaze of dawn's exultant light
Burst through the dark, had there not been
        a night?

Red Is the Earth

Red is the color of the pulsing earth—
The rouge of dawn across the night-paled sky;
The clamant radiance of the sunset dye;
Maroon of grief; sparkling cerise of mirth;
The spill of death; the tender surge of birth.
Red is the chalice wine to purity,
The heart's remembrance of its scarlet lie.
Wisdom is reckoned by the ruby's worth.

War sheds its crimson on the ravished land;
Red is the flaming color of desire;
Red is the tingling warmth in love's quick
    breath.
The red, young rose plucked by a careless
    hand,
Stained by earth's guilt, flushed with its sacred
    fire,
Holds for one moment all of life and death.

Total Triumph

There is that which ascends.
And if it ascends from noble height
It is glorious in flight;
But the bitter ounce of courage is not wrested
And the strength of splendid wing has no
    challenge to be tested.
Yet having ascended, it sits, lordly, on the
    predestined peak
In the silence of pride, preening its feathers
    with its beak.
But that which rises, self-chosen, from the flat
    land and the dust,
That which prevails over pinions short of
    spread and weak of thrust,
Inching upward, fighting lagging wing and
    leaden air,
Must brave with spirit alone what spirit alone
    will dare;
Must coax the listless clay a little onward
    toward that goal
Till even the indifferent currents must have
    mercy on its soul
And lift and hold the faltering wing a mite
Through chill of dawn, through desert day,
    through black
        and empty night—
O, when the peak is reached by that which
    must ascend or die
The whole world hears its flapping wing
And echoes even the echoes of its hoarse and
    joy-wrung cry!

The Sound of Silence

The sound that rises from unfathomed night
Falls, not upon the ear but on the soul
For it alone can sense such depth and height;
Can feel creation breathing as a whole.
This is the breath of eons yet unborn;
Of ages passed to time's decay and rust—
The chosen, the damned, the exalted, the
    forlorn
Inhaled, exhaled as dreams, fulfillment, dust.
The unhurried rhythm of creation fills
Night's caverned girth with mystic, pregnant
    air,
Breathing whatever destiny it wills
Upon the teeming silence waiting there.
Hear, in the rise and fall of night's deep
    breath,
The awesome rendezvous of life and death!

The Quickening Sands

Within each soul's vast country, land and tide,
Tall mountains rise and flowering meadows
blow;
But there are always deserts, deep and wide,
Across whose barren miles the soul must go.
A soul grows wise that thirsts in solitude;
That falls to rise and nurse, alone, its scars;
Whose desolate days have but an interlude
Of lonely nights beneath far, silent stars.
A soul grows great that toils through desert
land,
Seeing earth's bitter need revealed and bare;
Great with the burning urge to understand;
Great with the starlit stretch of heart to care.
Who once has wandered desert wastes alone
Must feel the thirst of others as his own.

Clock Watcher

Time is the little eye of mortal man
Judging how far and fast his lifetime goes.
He chains his actions to a rigid plan;
The tick of time is all he ever knows.
In minutes, hours and months and days
    and years
He moves to mechanize his life on earth;
The dial records the time he spends in tears;
A gong must end his measured hours of mirth.
Out in the vasty realm of cosmic space
Time is too small to set a measure on—
Just think how comes the night's unhurried
    pace!
And O, the sweet unfolding of the dawn!
If man could break his clock and wander free
He'd usher in his own infinity.

Grief

Grief captured me while I was dear and young
With apple blossoms sprinkled in my hair;
I had a song that needed to be sung;
I had a dream, a promise and a prayer.
But grief confined me to a doorless room
And sealed the windows in the walls of stone;
And there we groped in emptiness and gloom,
And there we drowsed, just grief and I alone.
But life drew near and roused me with its cry,
Its sharp command of stirring urgency;
In sudden, poignant wide-awakening I
Beat on my walls, demanding to be free!
A stone was loosened and I felt the mist
Of blowing night outside upon my skin;
And as I struck again with bleeding fist
The windows opened and the stars rushed in!

The Transient

Happiness comes when the eyes are not seeking;
Happiness comes when the bow is at rest;
It is a thing never pinioned or captured;
It is a thing never fully possessed.

Wealth cannot, love cannot, youth cannot give it;
Neither can age ever take it away;
It is not something you clutch like a penny;
And when you have it, be warned, it won't stay.

It is like mist with a pearl-tinted luster;
It is like wine when the vintage is right;
It is like dawn with the clean dew upon it;
It is like moonbeams that shimmer at night.

Gaze at it, glow with it, float on its vapor,
Daintily roll it about on the tongue,
Trip through its grasses with barefooted rapture,
Gather its cobwebs where dream-dust is hung.

Lightly, but lightly, with fingertips touch it—
Take but a breath that is carefully drawn—
Yet you are hardly aware that you have it
Till it has veiled itself, glimmered and gone.

The Heart Is the Beholder

I defined light as absence of the dark,
things cleared of denseness so the eyes could see
their contour, color, every visual mark.
The world I saw was then enough for me.
The days passed by, each day another day,
calm, captious, troubled—just the usual span.
I roamed the earth, saw life in every way,
thought I saw through the comedy of man.
And then love burst across the commonplace,
flooding with radiant fire my clockwork being,
shouting throughout my planet's ordered space
that I had never seen, for all my seeing.
Darkness, it showed me, is not just of night.
Dawn wakens from the heart—and love is light.

A White Lark Singing

Among the bitter, gray-shawled hours
When flesh succumbs and spirit cowers
As time ticks sad and old,
There darts across the drab of night
The lark with wings of moon-drenched white
And beak of polished gold.
He is the keeper of the dreams;
He sings of all the sweet extremes
The wish is conscious of.
He knows the gay and glittering touch
The heart deprived can crave so much—
Wealth, fame, excitement, love.
Behind my dreaming lids he sits;
Across my mind's free sky he flits—
My lark of gold and snow.
At dawn, of course he's never there,
But O my dears, I do not care.
At night I need him so!

World Patriot

Love is not contained
    and the urgency for the heart's stretch
       is the wind of God blowing.
Ocean meets ocean and sky meets sky
    and the sun is not caged
       behind little picket fences
        divided in its glowing.
The eye of the soul grows wide to behold
    the infinity of all things that be,
      more impartial than the sun, wider than
    the sky, deeper, fathoms deeper,
       than the waters under the sea.

How, then, can I say I love my son,
and not, by very loving,
love every mother's son?
How can I cry liberty! my liberty! and not cry
liberty
for each and every other one?
How can I cherish my red and human blood
with justifiable emotion
and not understand that blood meets blood
as ocean meets ocean?
I am my brother's keeper, and all creation
is my brother.
The anguish of a dying soldier is every man's
anguish,
one nation or another.
I am part of this land of the Stars and Stripes;
hers the arms that received me at birth.
Because she is my mother, my known and my
own, I love her above all the earth.
But picket fences cannot pen in
or portion out
little patches of the sun
and ocean meets ocean, sky meets sky
and blood meets blood as one.
It is written, I know, that until I revere
the proud freedom of every nation
and weep for its dying soldier
knowing we are one blood, one creation,
I shall not arrive at the sum of myself
nor feel the eye of the soul expand
nor love with the stretched heart's total love
my freedom,
my flag,
my land!

Stranger in the Night

Who walks so quietly across the night?
I hear the gentle crunch upon the snow
As this one passes. A dog's bark threatens,
Challenging the stranger. The sound of steps
Does not change rhythm—moves methodically
To some appointed destiny or goal.
Tomorrow I shall see the footprints there,
Not knowing whose they were or where he went
Or why he went or what awaited him.
Was he returning home to well-earned rest?
Was this a mission he was called upon?
Did he walk forth in anguish or despair?
The footprints he has left will not reveal
Such unimportant things. Nor will they show
If, secretly, he feared the barking dog.

Prayer for Childlike Faith

He patted seeds beneath the snow
and lisped that God would make them grow.
And God Who knows a wee one's needs
reached down and warmed the small,
    cold seeds.
Behold, in springtime's first bright hours
the child's seeds blossoming into flowers!

O, God of all infinity,
Who knows how wavering faith can be,
I know that You are All in All
but I feel weak and lost and small.
In this my chilling hour of need,
reach down and warm my winter seed!

Hour Twelve

I have been wound and set to the tick of earth,
   feeling its heartbeat beautiful in my veins.
I have followed its lure from the stroke of
   one—my birth—
lure of the sun, the winds and the sparkling
   rains
      all delights, all pains.
I have known grief and the cloister of long,
   numbed rest
      and paced bleak dawns in lonely awakening.
I have clutched new loves when old loves
   vanished, lest
my heart forget its lovely tryst with spring
   bursting! blossoming!
Let me never be wound and set to the loves ago,
   caught in the drowsy mist of memory
when the lure would lose its red, the tick turn
   slow;
when the winds and rains once lashing, fierce
   and free
      would lie soft for me.
There are dawns and darks ahead that have not
   been spent—
      I would not be spared earth's impulsive
         slash and scars.
If its ways are rash, then is rashness wonderment.
   When my heart can no longer strum its
      wild guitars
      let me be rewound and set to the tick of
         the stars!